KT-431-959

# RIVERS THROUGH TIME

# Settlements of the
# GANGES
## River

## Richard Spilsbury

**Heinemann** LIBRARY

JN 04314556

www.heinemann.co.uk/library
Visit our website to find out more information about **Heinemann Library** books.

To order:
☎ Phone 44 (0) 1865 888066
▤ Send a fax to 44 (0) 1865 314091
▣ Visit the Heinemann Bookshop at www.heinemann.co.uk/library to browse our catalogue and order online.

First published in Great Britain by Heinemann Library, Halley Court, Jordan Hill, Oxford OX2 8EJ, part of Harcourt Education.
Heinemann is a registered trademark of Harcourt Education Ltd.

© Harcourt Education Ltd 2004.
First published in paperback in 2006.
The moral right of the proprietor has been asserted.

All rights reserved. No part of this publication may be reproduced, stored in a retrieval system, or transmitted in any form or by any means, electronic, mechanical, photocopying, recording, or otherwise, without either the prior written permission of the publishers or a licence permitting restricted copying in the United Kingdom issued by the Copyright Licensing Agency Ltd, 90 Tottenham Court Road, London W1T 4LP (www.cla.co.uk).

Editorial: Jilly Attwood and Kate Bellamy
Design: Richard Parker and
        Tinstar Design Ltd (www.tinstar.co.uk)
Picture Research: Ruth Blair and Ginny Stroud-Lewis
Production: Séverine Ribierre
Originated by Dot Gradations
Printed in China by WKT Company Limited

| LINCOLNSHIRE COUNTY COUNCIL | |
| --- | --- |
| 04314556 | |
| PETERS | £8.25 |
| 06-Feb-08 | 954.1 |
| | |

**British Library Cataloguing in Publication Data**
Spilsbury, Richard
Settlements of the Ganges River –
    (Rivers through Time)
954.1
A full catalogue record for this book is available from the British Library.

Acknowledgements
The publishers would like to thank the following for permission to reproduce photographs: Alamy p. 22; Ancient Art and Architecture pp. 25, 26; Art Directors/Trip p. 4 AURORA p. 42 (Peter Essick); Corbis p. 36; Corbis pp. 23 (Bennett Dean/Eye Ubiquitous), 32 (Colin Garratt), 12, 43 (Gavriel Jecan), 11 (Reuters); Dinodia pp. 13, 15, 21; Hutchinson Library pp. 5, 8, 28, 33, 37, 38, 40; ICEE p. 9 (Dr M A Haque) Illustrated London News p. 34; Impact Photos pp. 18, 19; James Davis Worldwide Travel Library p. 27; Mary Evans Picture Library p. 31; Panos Pictures p. 29 (Jean Leo Dugast) Sylvia Cordaiy p. 35; Travel Ink p. 17; Trip p. 41 (D Saunders).

Cover photograph of the Ganges River at Varanasi reproduced with permission of Sarah-Jane Cleland/Lonely Planet Images.

Disclaimer
All the Internet addresses (URLs) given in this book were valid at the time of going to press. However, due to the dynamic nature of the Internet, some addresses may have changed, or sites may have ceased to exist since publication. While the author and publishers regret any inconvenience this may cause readers, no responsibility for any such changes can be accepted by either the author or the publishers.

Every effort has been made to contact copyright holders of any material reproduced in this book. Any omissions will be rectified in subsequent printings if notice is given to the publishers.

The paper used to print this book comes from sustainable resources.

# Contents

Words in bold, **like this,** are explained in the Glossary.

# Introducing the Ganges River

The Ganges is the longest river in the Indian **subcontinent**. Over its 2500 kilometre (1554 miles) length, the Ganges drops 4 kilometres (2 and a half miles) in height from its mountain **source**, down to the wide **delta** where it meets the sea. Nearly one tenth of the world's population live in the land around the Ganges and its **tributaries**. That's around 500 people for each square kilometre! They live in many different **settlements**, some with ancient histories that date back thousands of years.

## Legend of the Ganges

*In Hindu legend, a holy man burned 60,000 princes after they accused him of stealing a special horse belonging to their father, Sagara. The holy man told Sagara that only the Ganges River, which flowed in heaven, could save the princes' souls. Sagara's grandson, Bhagirath, prayed and the river started to pour to Earth from the god Vishnu's toe. Another god, Shiva, stopped the powerful river smashing the mountains as it landed by slowing the water's fall through his hair. Bhagirath led the Ganges from the Himalayas to the delta to wash over the princes ashes and into the sea (as depicted in this painting).*

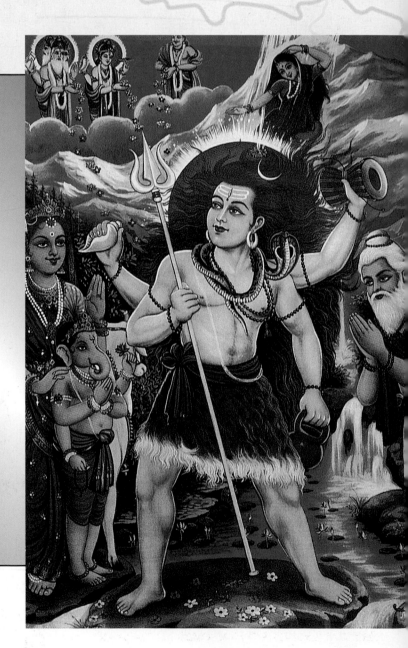

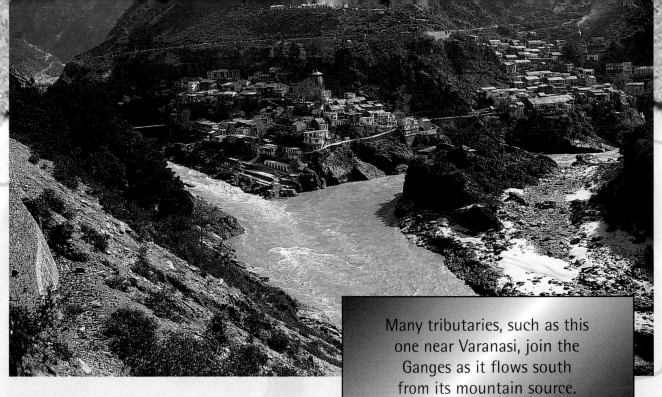

Many tributaries, such as this one near Varanasi, join the Ganges as it flows south from its mountain source.

## Holy river

The Ganges has a remarkable importance for many Indians as a holy river. Hindus believe the river is a goddess sent to Earth from Heaven. The goddess is called 'Ganga Maiya' or Mother Ganges. Water from the river, which gets it name from the goddess, is a vital part of many Hindu **rituals**. This has been a major factor in the growth of settlements along its **course**.

Like other rivers, settlements have developed along the Ganges because of its vital water supply. People, their animals and crops need fresh water to live and grow. Many industries, from fishing to **tanning** factories, rely on the river water. In the flat **plain** of the Ganges' middle **reaches**, there is only around 150cm (about 40 inches) of rain each year. Nearly all of this falls heavily in one short **monsoon** season. Yet the Ganges flows even in the hot,

dry season because it is fed by ice melting in the high mountains. This makes it an essential, permanent source of water. **Sediment** carried by the Ganges has washed onto the land making the soil fertile, which is ideal for farming.

### River terminology

*Confluence* – *the point where two rivers join.*

*Delta* – *where the river joins the sea.*

*Mouth* – *the ending point of a river.*

*Reaches* – *sections of the river (upper, middle and lower reaches).*

*River course* – *the path followed by a river from source to mouth.*

*Source* – *the starting point of a river.*

*Tributary* – *a river or stream that joins another (normally bigger) river.*

## The Ganges from source to mouth

The source of the Ganges is the Gangotri **glacier**, on the southern slopes of the Himalayan Mountains in the north of India. The glacier measures around 25 kilometres (about 15 miles) wide and spreads across several high valleys. The glacier's thick ice has formed from layers of snow that have fallen on top of each other over thousands of years. As more ice forms, it slips down the slopes incredibly slowly. When it falls to around 4000 metres above sea level, the lowest end melts because it becomes too warm for the water to remain frozen. This **meltwater** flows under the glacier and rushes from an ice cave at the end as a 30-metre (108-foot) wide, grey river. This is the Bhagirathi River. It becomes known as the Ganges 200 kilometres (124 miles) further down the mountains at the **confluence** with the Alaknanda River.

The upper reaches of the Bhagirathi and Ganges are fast flowing as they move downhill. The speed and strength of river water has **eroded** the softer rock of the Himalayas it has flowed over. The water has carved a deep river valley through the mountains.

After the Ganges leaves the mountains at the city of Haridwar, it enters the flat plains of north-east India. The river gets wider and **meanders**. It is dotted with **rapids** making boat **navigation** difficult down to Allahabad. In its middle reaches the Ganges is joined by several important tributaries that start in the Himalayas. These include the Yamuna, Gandak and Kosi Rivers.

At the border with Bangladesh, the Ganges turns south into its low-lying delta where it meets the Indian Ocean at the Bay of Bengal. The Ganges divides in two at the top of the delta. The Indian branch becomes the Hoogli River that flows past Kolkata. The other, larger, branch of the Ganges flows into Bangladesh, where it is called the Padma River. Here it joins with the Brahmaputra and Meghna Rivers. In the delta, the river flows slowly over flat land. As the river's speed slows, it drops sediment it has carried from upstream. Over a billion tonnes of sediment is deposited each year in the delta. This collects to form sandbanks and islands as the river water trickles towards the sea. River flow is stopped by seawater flowing inland at the coast. Sediment here has formed immense **estuaries**.

Map of the Ganges River from its source in the Himalayas to its mouth at the Bay of Bengal.

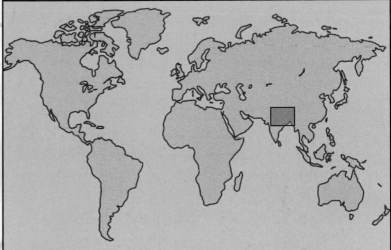

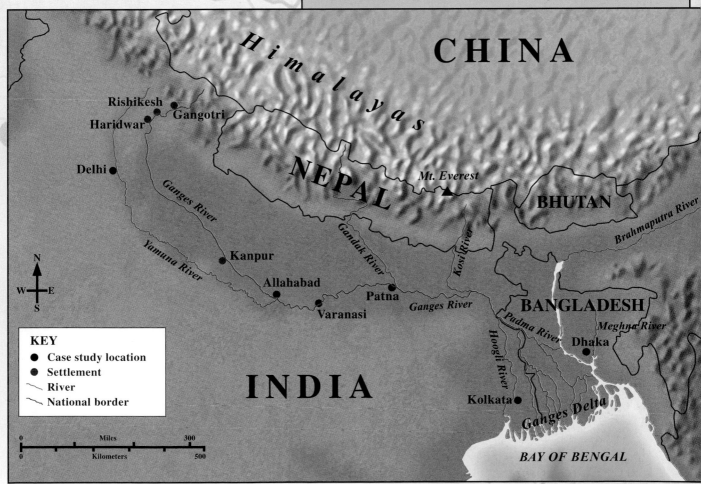

KEY
- ● Case study location
- ● Settlement
- ⌇ River
- ⌇ National border

## Settlements of the Ganges

The earliest settlements along the Ganges were generally small and temporary. Groups of **nomadic** herders brought their animals to drink the water of the Ganges, and to feed on riverside plants. Hunters came to catch fish, and trade the meat and skins of animals they had hunted in forests along the river. Other people came to the river because of its religious importance. Over time, farmers cleared land along the Ganges for **agriculture**. As there were not yet railways or roads, communities used the river where possible to transport surplus goods to other settlements. Larger settlements have grown along the Ganges since around 1500 BC.

The position of settlements along the Ganges has been affected by the shape or form of the landscape around the river. Along the high, steep Himalayan valleys of the upper reaches the land is covered with snow and ice for half of the year. There are also few areas of flat land to farm and build on. Settlements have usually developed in more sheltered parts of the hills. Over the centuries, farmers have cut flat ledges called terraces into many of the

Terraced fields provide agricultural land for mountain communities.

Kanpur is sometimes known as the 'Manchester of India'. This is because, like Manchester in the UK, it has grown important as a large industrial centre, supplied by the waters from the river.

hillsides along the Ganges. Remote settlements such as Gaumukh, at the base of the Gangotri glacier, have grown because they are places of **pilgrimage** for Hindus.

Travelling south-east from the city of Haridwar, where the river leaves the mountains, the Ganges enters the flat plains of its middle and lower reaches. Crops such as wheat, cotton, and rice, grow quickly on the banks of extensive farmland between the Ganges and its tributaries. The soil is fertile because the **nutrients** in the sediment are washed onto the land by the river, and the climate is warmer and drier. These fields provide food for the huge population of the plains. Along the middle reaches and tributaries are the big cities of Delhi, Allahabad, Varanasi and Patna. As

the Ganges moves into its delta, large areas of low-lying land are flooded for parts of the year. This region is home to two of the largest settlements on the Ganges, Kolkata and Dhaka.

In this book we will explore some of the significant settlements of the Ganges River. Our journey through time starts with Allahabad, founded over 4000 years ago, and ends with Bangladesh's modern capital city, Dhaka. We will look at why each settlement was founded where it was, how it has changed and what it might be like in the future. How are settlements linked to the Ganges River, and how has the importance of the region and the river changed over time?

# Allahabad: meeting point

## Earliest Prayaga

Allahabad was one of the earliest major settlements of the Ganges. Its original name, Prayaga, means meeting point of rivers. Prayaga was first established on the Ganges over 4000 years ago. Water was very important in the religious ceremonies of the Dasa people, India's original inhabitants. There are descriptions of ancient Dasa river festivals in famous Indian poems and stories, such as the *Vedas* and *Mahabharata*, that date back as early as 1000 BC. In these **rituals**, worshippers dipped pots of dry grain into the river to soak it before sowing. This helped the seeds **germinate**. The worshippers saw the river as a giver of life.

Prayaga was also a meeting point between the Dasa and **migrants**, called the Aryans. The Aryans were a group of people from northern Asia who migrated into what is now Pakistan and then into the Ganges **basin** from around 1500 BC. Aryans brought several new things to India with them. These included a language called Sanskrit, horse-drawn chariots, herds of cattle, painted pottery, and beliefs about how society should be organized.

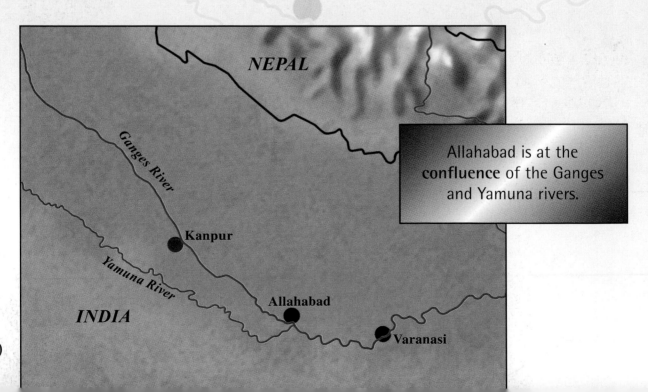

Allahabad is at the **confluence** of the Ganges and Yamuna rivers.

As Aryans lived alongside the Dasa, a new cultural mix spread through India from Prayaga and eastwards along the Ganges. The **Hindu** religion, as we know it today, first developed at this time, with its beliefs about the use of special priests, public religious ceremonies and many different gods. The Hindu belief that cows are sacred, which is still held today, may also date from the Aryans. As great traders in cattle, cows meant wealth and importance to the Aryans. As a result, cattle theft became a major source of conflict between people.

## Abode of God

Prayaga also grew into a thriving centre for boat-building and other trade in the region. Whoever controlled Prayaga could control transport down the Yamuna and Ganges Rivers and on towards the Ganges' **delta**. In AD 1575, the **Muslim** ruler of the northern half of India, Emperor Akbar, took control of the city. He renamed it Illahabas, later called Allahabad, which means abode of god. Akbar built a giant stone fort on a strategic point overlooking the Ganges in 1583, so that his troops could defend the city.

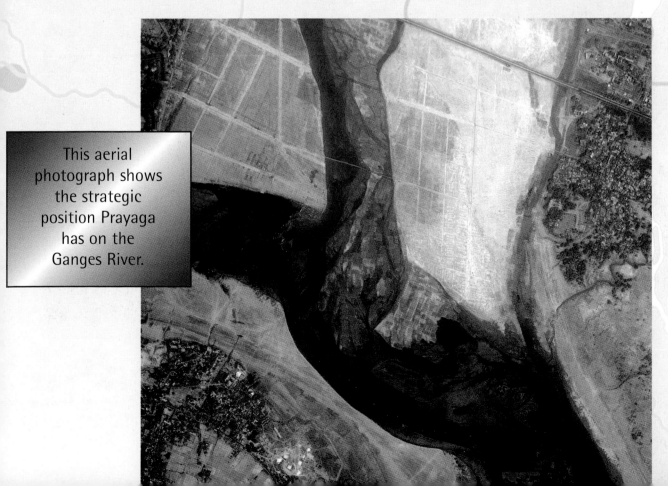

This aerial photograph shows the strategic position Prayaga has on the Ganges River.

## Kumbh Mela

*For most Hindus, bathing in holy river water is a vital part of their religion. They believe it will cleanse them and their **ancestors** of any wrongdoings in the past and help them on their way to heaven. Ganges water at Allahabad is prized because Hindus believe it is the meeting point of three holy rivers: the Ganges, the Yamuna, and the mythical underground river, the Saraswati.*

*As the Ganges at Allahabad is considered so holy, one of the greatest religious festivals in India, the Kumbh Mela, happens there in January and February, once every 12 years. Pilgrims travel from all over India and other parts of the world for the Kumbh Mela. Around 30 million people visited the 2001 Kumbh Mela, making it probably the largest gathering in history! Some stay in Allahabad's hotels, but most camp in tents on the riverbank. They bathe in the river and often chant 'Jai Ganga Maiya', 'Long live mother Ganga'. They also pray, listen to concerts, give money or food to the needy and receive blessings from holy men such as **saddhus**.*

| c.4000 BC | c.1500 BC | AD c.350 |
|---|---|---|
| Earliest records of Prayaga on Ganges. | Aryans arrive in Prayaga. | Prayaga is a major settlement ruled by Gupta emperors. |

Allahabad University, built by British rulers, was the largest university in India in the early 1900s. It remains an educational centre of the Ganges.

**FACT**

Four Indian prime ministers were born and educated in Allahabad, including Jawaharlal Nehru, the first Prime Minister of India.

## Religion and learning

Allahabad also became a centre of learning on the Ganges. People wanted to calculate when religious festivals along the river should happen, and when they should plant crops. They studied maths and astronomy to help them choose the best times. Emperor Akbar was also influential in developing Allahabad. He tried to start a new religion based on **Islam** and Hinduism. So, he asked scholars to translate and copy Hindu poems and tales to spread around his Muslim empire. Allahabad developed into a place where people with different beliefs met and exchanged ideas.

## Great rebellion

The British took control of Allahabad from its Muslim leaders in 1801. During the next century and a half, people in Allahabad struggled to get rid of their foreign occupiers. In 1857 the **Great Rebellion**, or Indian Mutiny, started near Delhi. Indian troops working for the British army had refused to use new rifles. This was because the bullets contained animal fat that it was against their religions to touch. News of this rebellion spread westwards along the Ganges. At Allahabad, Indian rebels briefly took control of Akbar's fort from British soldiers. The Great Rebellion showed Indians that independence from the **British Empire** was possible.

| **1575** | **1801** | **1857** |
|---|---|---|
| Akbar renames Prayaga Illahabas (Allahabad). | British take over Allahabad. | Great Rebellion (Indian Mutiny). |

# Varanasi: sacred city

## City of light

Varanasi is one of the most sacred cities in India for **Hindus**. It has been a religious centre for over 2500 years. Varanasi was originally called Kashi, which means 'to shine'. Hindus believe **Brahman** lights up their path to Heaven from Varanasi. Unusually, at Varanasi the Ganges flows north towards its **source**, rather than south-east towards its **delta**. Hindus consider the source of the Ganges to be a sacred place, as it is where the goddess Ganga came to Earth. They also believe that Varanasi is where the God Shiva made his home on Earth. All Hindus try to visit Varanasi at least once in their life.

### Hinduism in brief

*Hindus believe their soul, or spirit, lives on after they die. The soul then moves to become part of a new living form, as a human, animal or plant. When that life ends, the soul moves on again. This endless cycle of birth and death is called **reincarnation**. A Hindu's ultimate wish is to escape reincarnation and for their soul to become part of Brahman. To help this, they pray to gods, visit holy places and do good deeds. Over three-quarters of all Indians are Hindus.*

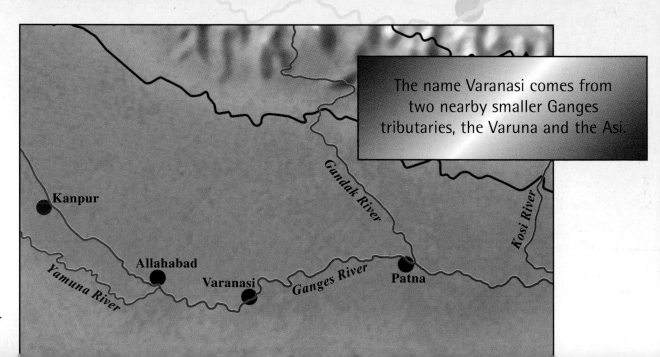

The name Varanasi comes from two nearby smaller Ganges tributaries, the Varuna and the Asi.

Kanpur

Allahabad

Varanasi

Patna

*Gandak River*

*Kosi River*

*Yamuna River*

*Ganges River*

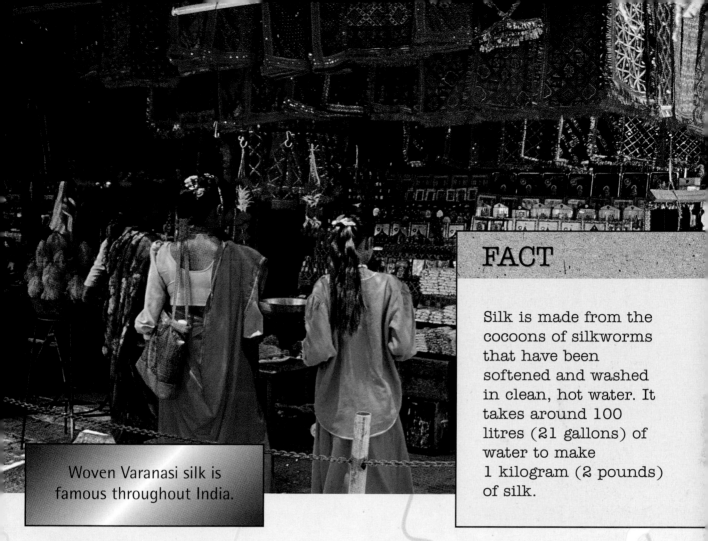

Woven Varanasi silk is famous throughout India.

# FACT

Silk is made from the cocoons of silkworms that have been softened and washed in clean, hot water. It takes around 100 litres (21 gallons) of water to make 1 kilogram (2 pounds) of silk.

## Varanasi develops

The area around Varanasi is important for **Buddhists**, too. Sarnath, just 10 kilometres (6 miles) from the city, is where Buddhists believe the Buddha lived for a while. Buddhist **pilgrims** from China first visited the area as early as AD 640. These visitors also brought **silkworms** to the area.

The Ganges helped Varanasi become a major silk producer. It was used in silk production and to transport the cloth. Silk traders became rich and built grand temples and places of learning. Varanasi University is still a major centre for the study of Sanskrit, the language used to write the earliest Hindu holy books.

In 1194, the forces of the **Muslim** ruler, Muhammad of Ghor, took over Varanasi. They destroyed Hindu temples, partly to reuse the stones to build **mosques**, smashed statues of gods and carried away hundreds of camel-loads of treasure. Later rulers, such as the Muslim emperor Akbar, in the 16th century, and British colonizers in the 18th and 19th centuries, were more tolerant of Hinduism. Varanasi was gradually rebuilt and remained an independent city state until 1949.

## Ghats and temples

Wide stone steps run along the Ganges for nearly seven kilometres (about four miles) through Varanasi. These steps are called **ghats**. They were built to allow pilgrims to get to the water easily from the temples and streets above. Most of the 84 ghats have a special importance for different bathers. Some were built for private use by important people and their families whereas others were built for particular communities of Hindus. For example, Nishadraj ghat is a lucky bathing place for boatmen and fishermen. A few ghats are also specially set aside as places to burn the dead.

The ghats are always teeming with people. There are not only thousands of visitors but also priests, **saddhus**, beggars and fortune-tellers. Stallholders sell food or offerings such as butter or flowers used in religious rituals. Many visitors take boat trips on the Ganges to pray and watch the activities on the banks.

There are 1500 temples in Varanasi. Many are tiny, simple, and dimly lit. Others are large and grand. They tower over the river, and can be seen from all around. Some temples are only open to particular groups of Hindus, others to any worshipper. Each is dedicated to a different god or goddess. The Golden temple, dedicated to Shiva, was originally built around 1600. Although it was knocked down and covered with a mosque by Muslim rulers, it was extravagantly rebuilt in 1776. The temple gets its name from the three-quarters of a tonne of gold that coats its surface!

Each day around 70,000 people
come to Varanasi to bathe in the
Ganges, visit temples and see the
sights. Some have giant parasols
to shelter them from the hot Sun.

17

## Cremation

Hindus believe the best place to die is at Varanasi. They cremate their dead on the special ghats and scatter the ashes on the Ganges. In this way people hope to reduce the number of times they are reincarnated. The people who cremate bodies at Varanasi are the Doms, one group of the **dalits** (see box). Doms build a funeral pyre out of logs, coconuts, and reeds. They show the dead person's family how to light the wood, and then stay close to the fire to make sure it does not go out. It takes about three hours for Doms to burn each body and then collect the ashes for the family. At Varanasi, around 250 people are cremated each day.

## Hindu society

*Traditionally all Hindu people were divided into five major groups based on their ancestors and roles in society. The most important group, or caste, is the priests. Next most important are rulers and soldiers, then traders and professionals, and then labourers and servants. The people with least power are the dalits or untouchables. In the past, people from important castes were not allowed to work, eat or make friends with dalits.*

People pay around 500 rupees to Doms for each cremation on the burning ghats at Varanasi. That's only about £6.

| c.600 BC | AD 1194 |
|---|---|
| Varanasi is established as a religious centre. | Muhammed of Ghori takes over and destroys Varanasi. |

## Polluted Ganges

The Ganges is badly polluted. Unfortunately, when people bathe in or drink Ganges water at Varanasi they also risk getting ill. Waste, such as chemicals from silk factories, and even corpses that families cannot afford to cremate, are dumped in the river. The city's **sewage** system cannot cope with the volume of waste produced by all its visitors. It was built in 1917 when the population was much smaller. Newer factories built to clean up sewage are broken. About 10 million litres (about 2640 thousand gallons) of sewage flows into the Ganges at Varanasi each hour. This is enough to fill 12 Olympic-sized swimming pools!

Scientists have discovered that the Ganges is faster than most rivers at breaking down sewage. Nevertheless, the problem is getting worse. Many Hindus cannot accept that the river is getting too dirty to use in their rituals.

## FACTS

Drinking water in Varanasi is 10,000 times more polluted with disease-causing bacteria than recommended levels. One person in the Ganges region dies each minute from diarrhoea, a disease that can be caused by drinking polluted water.

| c.1750 | 1917 | 1949 |
|---|---|---|
| Varanasi becomes an independent state within India; many temples and ghats built. | Sewage system built. | Varanasi becomes part of Indian state of Uttar Pradesh. |

# Patna: capital of the first empire of India

## Mauryan Empire

Patna is now the capital of Bihar state and a major city of the Ganges. It was once called Pataliputra, and was the capital of an empire covering nearly the whole of India.

By 600 BC, much of the land around the middle **reaches** of the Ganges had been settled. Iron tools, which were vital in this process, were made from the large amount of valuable **iron ore** that was mined and traded in Bihar state. Rival chieftains battled to control trade along the Ganges as they realized the strategic importance of the river. By 325 BC a clear leader of the region had emerged, named Chandragupta Maurya.

Chandragupta built his capital city, Pataliputra, on the site of a small fort overlooking the river. He developed a city of palaces, a university, gardens, temples and markets. Chandragupta liked to have direct control over his empire. He used government workers and spies to help him manage his people. Chandragupta grew his empire through war, and also through negotiation. In 305 BC he bought the Indus valley in northwest India for 500 elephants!

Patna lies just upstream of the confluence with the Gandak River.

## New order

Chandragupta Maurya gave up power in 301 BC and his son Bindusara reigned. One of Bindusara's sons, Asoka, then ruled from 269 BC. Asoka became more and more upset by the battles to control and expand the Mauryan Empire. Asoka also became attracted to **Buddhist** beliefs. Under Asoka, the Mauryan Empire changed to become a more peaceful and tolerant place.

Asoka spread his Buddhist beliefs through his empire by having them inscribed in local languages on stone pillars.

## Buddhism in brief

*Buddhism was founded in India in the 6th century BC by an Indian prince called Siddhartha Gautama. Buddhism is a religion without a god. Instead, Buddhists follow the teachings of Gautama, who is also known as Buddha. After much travelling, Gautama believed he had discovered how to achieve a state of perfect peace, under a special tree at Bodhgaya, near present-day Patna. He taught others, and his followers have spread his beliefs of decency, mercy and truthfulness since then.*

## Pataliputra

The Ganges remained a vital way of transporting heavy goods through the empire. Pataliputra was an important port and ferry crossing point across the Ganges, which is several kilometres wide here. The government in Pataliputra controlled trade not only in Indian goods, but also those arriving in India by sea, such as rare woods, spices, gemstones, and precious metals from the Middle East.

During Asoka's 37-year reign, Pataliputra was the largest city in the world with a population of up to 300,000. He built free hospitals, beautiful palaces and developed a new language called Prakrit. Asoka got rid of troops and consulted with people about new laws. At its height, the Mauryan Empire stretched from the Bay of Bengal to the Arabian Sea. Asoka's **edicts** have been found in Afghanistan, Nepal, and southern India.

The Mahatma Gandhi Setu Bridge, joining Patna to Hajipur, was built in 1982. It is one of the world's longest river bridges at 7.5 kilometres (4.5 miles).

| 63 BC | 325 | 301–269 |
|---|---|---|
| Gotama (Buddha) born. | Chandragupta becomes ruler of Mauryan Empire. | Bindusara reigns. |

## Patna rice

*For a long time, almost all good-quality, large-grained rice from India was called Patna rice. This is because the fertile land around Patna was the main rice-growing region. Rice plants grow best in warm places with their roots underwater. Around Patna the low-lying land floods during the **monsoon** and also when **irrigated** with river water during drier parts of the year. Today Patna rice is grown around the world.*

After Asoka died in 232 BC, the empire started to break up. Pataliputra remained the major city in the region for another four centuries, but then fell into ruin. Today, there are just a few remains of Mauryan buildings at Kumrahar, not far from the local railway station.

## New city

The fortunes of this Ganges **settlement** improved when it became the centre of the **Muslim** kingdom of Sher Shah Suri in 1545. The new city was named Azimabad, and later Patna. Today, Patna sprawls for 16 kilometres (10 miles) along the curving southern bank of the river. Its population is nearly 2 million. It is an **agricultural** centre for crops such as rice, sesame, and sugar cane. It is also a stopping off and crossing point for visitors moving to and from Nepal, a few hundred kilometres to the north.

| 269–232 | AD 319–500 | 1540–5 | 1982 |
|---|---|---|---|
| Reign of Asoka. | Gupta empire. | Azimabad (later Patna) built on site of Pataliputra. | New road bridge called the Mahatma Gandhi Setu built across Ganges. |

# Delhi: changing capital

## Earliest cities of Delhi

Delhi lies on the Yamuna River, a major **tributary** of the Ganges. The city gets its name from Dhillika, the earliest village at this site on the Yamuna River, but the first major **settlement** here was called Indraprastha. This was started as early as 1000 BC. In 1206 **Muslim** invaders from central Asia, attracted by the wealth of India, established a new state called the Delhi Sultanate. Over the following centuries, successive rulers of the Sultanate built new cities at Delhi, each grander than the previous one. Ferozabad, founded in 1354 was once the richest city in the world. All that is left of it today is a ruined palace.

## FACT

Some scientists believe the Yamuna once flowed westwards toward the Arabian Sea. Since then, the height of the land around the river has changed. This has caused the Yamuna to turn eastwards, joining with the Ganges.

Delhi is well placed as a trade and communication route between India's neighbouring countries, Pakistan and Nepal. It also has rich farmland between the Ganges and Yamuna, where wheat and cotton thrive.

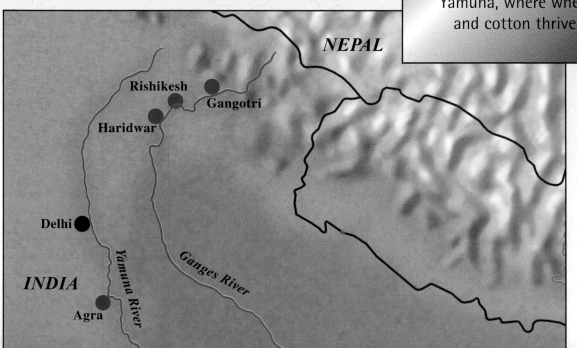

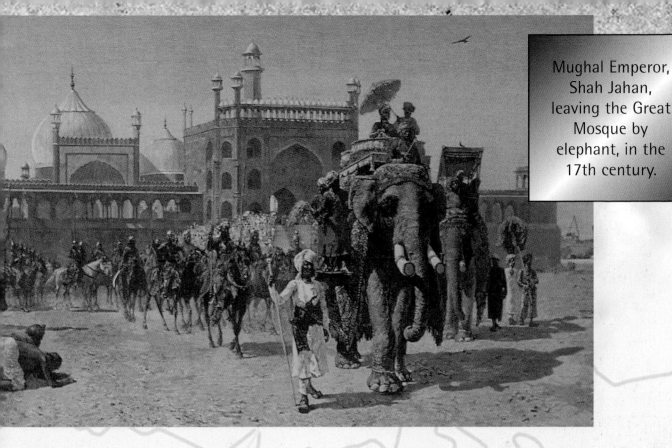

Mughal Emperor, Shah Jahan, leaving the Great Mosque by elephant, in the 17th century.

# From sultans to Mughals

The ruling Muslim sultans raided many parts of India to get rich. In 1310, for example, the conquering army of Ala-ud-din, or Aladdin, returned to Delhi from southern India. They had plundered 612 elephants, over 200 tonnes of gold from temples, 20,000 horses, and caskets of jewels. The Sultanate used some of their wealth to build elaborate mosques in Delhi including the famous prayer tower of Qutab Minar. The sultans' power started to break up when local rulers began establishing their own kingdoms.

In 1526, Babur seized Delhi in a bloody battle. Babur was the first of the Mughal emperors. Babur's grandson, Akbar, was considered the greatest of the Mughal emperors. Akbar allowed local rulers to have some power. In return, the rulers gave him soldiers, elephants, and some of his 300 wives!

## New to India

*The Sultanate imported new goods into Delhi and the rest of India. Paper, from Iran, rapidly replaced palm leaves to write on, and books helped spread ideas. The spinning wheel, also from central Asia, speeded up production of cotton cloth. India became a major cotton exporter. A final arrival, gunpowder from China, changed the way wars were fought throughout the country.*

The thick sandstone walls of Shah Jahan's Red Fort protected his army and imperial palace.

## River fortresses

The Mughal emperors used the Yamuna River as protection. By building fortresses on the bend of the river, they could see approaching enemies from far off and rely on the river to slow any attacks. Akbar moved his capital to the already fortified city of Agra, 200 kilometres (124 miles) from Delhi, overlooking the Yamuna. In 1571 he ordered a completely new capital called Fatehpur Sikri to be built. This was 40 kilometres (26 miles) from the river on a spot where a local priest had predicted good luck for Akbar. After only 14 years Akbar abandoned his capital, partly because it had a poor water supply, but mostly because it was unprotected from possible invaders. Akbar returned to the safety of Agra.

In 1638, Shah Jahan, Akbar's grandson, started to build a new capital in Delhi, just north of where Indraprastha had stood. This was called Shahjahanabad but we know it today as Old Delhi. Old Delhi was completely enclosed in thick stone walls up to 33 metres (108 feet) high. Soldiers kept watch from 27 towers and controlled movement in and out of the city using 14 gates.

## Love token

*Shah Jahan ordered the beautiful white marble Taj Mahal at Agra to be built in memory of his dead wife. It took 20,000 people, around 20 years to build. After he was replaced by his son as emperor, Shah Jahan spent the last years of his life in prison in Agra fort and had a perfect view of his creation.*

## Old Delhi

Old Delhi was planned as a spacious city with gardens and canals between the buildings and streets. The canals brought water from the Yamuna River into the city. This was needed because city wells were beginning to dry up. It was also used to fill the many baths and fountains in Shah Jahan's lavish palace. Old Delhi's riches attracted merchants and craftsmen who set up shops in **bazaars**. Each bazaar was home to a different set of shopkeepers, from spice merchants to barbers. Chandni Chowk, in the centre of Old Delhi, means Silver Street. This name is believed to come from either the canals that ran down the street, reflecting the moonlight, or from the silver jewellery made and sold there.

Chandni Chowk was one of the richest streets in the world during Shah Jahan's reign. Today it is still a place to buy goods such as jewels, perfumes and flowers.

# From Old to New Delhi

In the early 19th century Delhi was taken over by British forces. Whereas the capital of the Mughal empire was Delhi, the British governed the whole of India from Kolkata on the Ganges **delta**. Delhi became a less important Indian city. Neglected, some of the streets of Old Delhi fell to ruin. The formerly clear canals fed by the Yamuna River filled with rubbish and turned to murky pools where disease-carrying insects bred.

The city regained its importance in the late 19th century as the British expanded the railway. Around 14,000 kilometres (9000 miles) of tracks had been laid in India by 1880. The railway meant people could get around quicker, in greater numbers, all over the country. Goods could be transported in bulk and over long distances. Delhi became a central point controlling journeys in all directions. In 1911 the British King, George V, visited the city and decided to make Delhi the capital of British India. British architects were employed to enlarge the city. The new areas were similar to those in London at the time. This part of the city is known as New Delhi.

New Delhi was carefully planned, with broad tree-lined avenues and grand government buildings.

| AD c.300 | 1206 | 1648 |
|---|---|---|
| First city of Delhi, Indraprastha, built. | Delhi sultanate established. | Capital of Mughal empire, Shahjahanabad, or Old Delhi, completed. |

## Riverside slums

*Yamuna pushta is one of Delhi's thousands of **slum** settlements on the banks of the Yamuna River. Tens of thousands of poor people live here as there is not enough cheap housing in the city. The river here is filled with sewage and rubbish. Half of all Delhi's sewage is pumped untreated into the Yamuna river. But it is the only water available for the people living in the slums. When people drink dirty water they can catch infectious diseases that can cause illnesses, like diarrhoea.*

## Modern Delhi

Today, Delhi is the capital of independent India. It is changing quickly. Its traditional mill industries, powered by water from the Yamuna River, are now being replaced with hi-tech industries, such as foreign computer companies.

Many people move into Delhi from around India, hoping to find work. The growing population is putting a serious strain on the city's water resources. Most of Delhi's water comes from the Yamuna River, the rest from **groundwater** supplies. Both water resources are badly polluted. Delhi's citizens require around 3 million litres (about 79 thousand gallons) of clean water each day, for example to drink or flush toilets with. However, they get about two thirds of this because water cleaning and pumping systems are too slow and water is lost through broken pipes.

| 1803 | 1931 | 1950 |
|---|---|---|
| British take over Delhi. | New Delhi completed as official capital of British India. | Delhi is made the official capital of independent India. |

# Kolkata: gateway to East India

## Foreign interests

Kolkata is the major Indian settlement of the Ganges **delta**. Today it is home to around 13 million people. But it only came into being as an important **settlement** 300 years ago, as the gateway to East India. In the 16th and 17th centuries, the Mughal empire started to allow private Portuguese, Dutch, Danish, French, and British merchants to set up **trading colonies** around the coast of India. The European name for Asia in those days was the East Indies, so these colonies were called the East India Companies. The Indian rulers wanted gold and silver, mostly from America, to make coins and to decorate their palaces. The Europeans wanted fine quality silk and cotton fabrics, and indigo, a dye made from indigo (indigoferra) plants growing in the Ganges delta.

## FACT

Indigo was in great demand to dye the British navy's uniforms dark blue. The colour became known as navy blue.

The companies set up warehouses where they could store their goods until they could be shipped to Europe. They formed their own private armies, equipped with up-to-date European weapons, to protect their goods. Local rulers began to employ the companies' armies to fight their battles and the company leaders became richer and more respected in return.

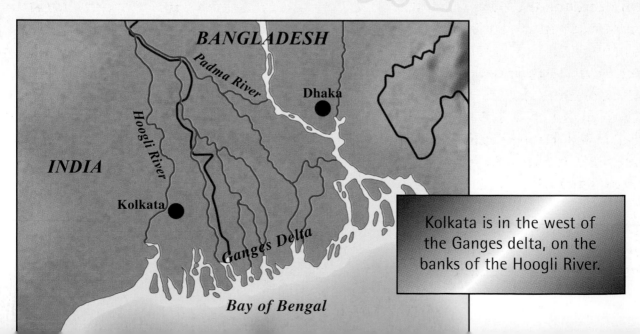

Kolkata is in the west of the Ganges delta, on the banks of the Hoogli River.

In the late 18th century, around 200,000 people were living in Kolkata.

# Birth of a city

By the late 17th century, the growing British East India Company wanted a permanent site on the Hoogli River, connected to the Ganges. In 1690, an employee called Job Charnock set up a factory in three tiny villages, at a deep part of the river. Of the three village names, Sutanuti, Kalikata, and Govindapur, it was the name Kalikata that stuck for the settlement. Kalikata later became Calcutta and is now known as Kolkata.

The British East India Company made Kolkata the centre of their activities in eastern India and a town grew around the factory. However, others wanted to take control of this thriving spot. In 1756 the forces of a local ruler, Siraj, attacked. Most European residents fled the town, but about 60 were imprisoned in a small cellar in the fort. About 40 of these people suffocated. This incident became known as 'the Black Hole of Calcutta'. It prompted the British to retake Kolkata, defeat Siraj and his forces at the Battle of Plassey, and build a better fort to defend the town. In 1773 Kolkata became the capital of all the British East India Company's territories.

## Home from home

In 1858, the British government took control of the riches of the East India Company. India was the biggest part of the global **British Empire**. Kolkata, its capital, was now second only to London in importance. For the many British who came to work there, Kolkata offered comforts they were used to back home. By the late 19th century, unlike most Indian cities, Kolkata had sewers, a filtered water supply, a cathedral, trams, cricket grounds, and even a golf course.

## River link

The port of Kolkata was the most important in India in the 18th to 19th centuries. It was the link between the middle and lower **reaches** of the Ganges, and neighbouring countries, such as Nepal, and the rest of the world. Until the 18th century, the Ganges was deep enough for large boats to **navigate** as far as Allahabad. Since then the river has become clogged with **sediment**.

The arrival of the steam engine in the mid-1800s also brought changes to river transport. Faster **steamships** could move up the Hoogli and across the Bay of Bengal from Kolkata. However, they needed huge amounts of coal for fuel so the railway was used to connect Kolkata to nearby inland coalfields. Rail transport for bulky goods, such as coal and cotton, soon took over from river transport as it was quicker and more economical.

Today around 10 percent of India's imports and exports pass through Kolkata port.

# The story of jute

Jute is a plant that has been used in India for centuries for making thread to weave into hard-wearing cloth. Jute grows very fast in the hot, damp climate of the Ganges delta. Four-month-old plants are cut and softened by soaking in river water. Then their long, tough fibres are pulled out and dried in the sun before they are ready to use.

In the early 19th century, hemp and linen cloth were becoming expensive as the raw materials they were made from were in short supply. The British East India Company realized jute cloth could be a good substitute but it could not be made quickly or cheaply enough on hand **looms** in India. At first they sent jute yarn to Dundee, Scotland, where steam-powered hemp looms were used to make it into cloth. In 1855 jute cloth started to be produced by mechanical looms in Kolkata. Jute mills sprang up along the western side of the Hoogli River. The mills used coal transported by the trains, and river water to power the looms. They were built by deep docks where large ships could be loaded with cloth for **export**. In 1869, there were 5 mills with 950 looms. By 1910, Kolkata's 30,000 looms were producing a billion metres (about 1.1 billion yards) of jute cloth and hundreds of millions of jute bags.

Even though synthetic fibres have increasingly replaced jute, it remains a significant Kolkata export, especially in times of war when it is used to make sand bags.

33

In Bengal, at Partition, millions of people migrated to areas that matched their religion.

## Into the 20th century

Most Indians resented British rule of their country and wanted an independent country governed by Indians. Kolkata became a major centre of protest in the independence movement. In 1885 the Indian National Congress, the first political party for all Indians, was formed in Kolkata. Some Hindus suggested the British had only become rulers because they had been helped by the Muslim Mughal empire.

In 1905, after fighting between Hindus and Muslims, the British divided Bengal in two based on the most common religion in each part. The boundary separated Hindu West Bengal, including Kolkata, and Muslim East Bengal. Bengali people were so angry about this forced division, that the British had to uproot their capital from Kolkata to Delhi in 1911.

When India finally gained independence from British rule in 1947 it split into Muslim Pakistan, including East Bengal, and mostly Hindu India. This was called **Partition**.

| 1690 | 1756 | 1855 | 1877 |
|------|------|------|------|
| Beginnings of Kolkata, factory at Sutanuti. | 'Black hole of Calcutta' incident. | First jute mill in Kolkata. | Kolkata is capital of the British Empire. |

## Independent Kolkata

After Partition the newly arrived refugees in Kolkata put great stress on the city's resources. There were widescale food shortages and thousands lived on the streets. There was a shortage of raw materials for jute mills, as the main jute growing areas were now part of Pakistan, so many workers lost their jobs.

Kolkata's position on the river means it remains a busy port city today. The city is a centre of independent thought, and home to a distinctive Bengali **culture**. Its grand buildings stand as a reminder of the days when it was at the heart of the British Empire.

## Keeping the Hoogli open

*Sediment has gradually filled in the Hoogli River in Kolkata, preventing large ships reaching the ports. So, the Indian government built the Farakka Barrage (see below) across the Ganges to divert Ganges water into the Hoogli. This means the ports can stay open, even in the dry season before the monsoon rains fill the river. The barrage is just upriver of where the Hoogli splits off the Ganges and where Bangladesh begins. This has caused arguments between India and Bangladesh as it creates water shortages in Bangladesh.*

| **1885** | **1911** | **1947** | **1975** |
|---|---|---|---|
| India National Congress founded in Kolkata. | British move capital from Kolkata to New Delhi. | Partition of British India into India and Pakistan. | Farakka Barrage was finished on the Hoogli River. |

# Dhaka: megacity on the delta

Dhaka is the capital of the **Muslim** country, Bangladesh, on the Ganges **delta**. Dhaka was founded on the riches of the delta's **agriculture**. It was first established as a trading centre of the mughal Emperor Jehangir in 1608. Rice, cotton, jute, and silk are major exports today, as they were nearly 400 years ago.

## Birth of a new country

Dhaka was made capital of the state of East Bengal in 1905, which became East Pakistan after **Partition** in 1947. Muslim Pakistan had two parts, and East Pakistan was the larger.

### Shifting river

*The course of the Ganges through its delta has shifted over time. **Sediment** deposited by the river has blocked its passage in some directions and redirected it to flow in others. Dhaka lies on the banks of the Buriganga River. This river was once one course that part of the Ganges took to reach the Bay of Bengal. Today, the Buriganga is not connected to the Ganges but retains 'ganga' in its name.*

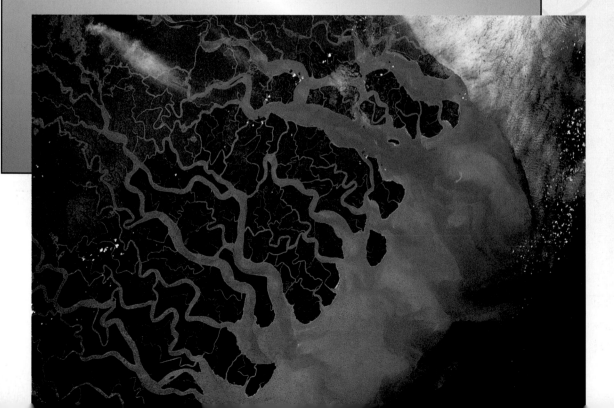

Dhaka is a mixture of old buildings from Mughal times, and new skyscrapers and parliament buildings.

However, rich leaders from smaller West Pakistan ran both parts. Muslims in larger, poorer East Pakistan wanted to be independent, and govern themselves. Sheikh Mujib, who led the independence movement, was put in jail by Pakistan's government in 1970. In March 1971, Rahman's supporters were protesting about his treatment, when the government sent their troops in, killing thousands. The government of India, who had fallen out with the government of Pakistan, stepped in to help Rahman's followers. In December 1971, war broke out between India and Pakistan, in which three million people died. At the end of the war East Pakistan became its own independent country, Bangladesh, with Dhaka as its capital.

## FACT

Dhaka's prized cotton fabrics are known as muslin. It may be that the word comes from an accidental change to the word, Muslim, the name of the city's major religion.

## Dhaka today

Most of Dhaka was rebuilt after the war. There are over 700 **mosques** and other religious buildings for the city's worshippers. Coastal estuaries south of Dhaka have created new wealth for Bangladesh. Natural gas, a valuable fuel, can be found under the delta sediments. Dhaka has also developed as a centre for the clothing trade, **exporting** from ports on the mouth of the Ganges.

In 1998, over half of Dhaka was flooded, making nearly a quarter of a million people homeless.

## Flooding in Bangladesh

The whole of Bangladesh is very vulnerable to flooding as the land is generally low-lying and flat. Each year up to 40 percent of the country is usually flooded during the **monsoon**. The monsoon rainclouds blow in from the Indian Ocean between June and October. Monsoon rains falling in the Ganges **basin** raise water levels in the Ganges and its delta. Normally 1.5 metres (5 feet) of rain falls on Bangladesh. All this extra water causes rivers and lakes to swell and overflow.

Dhaka, like any other big city, relies on services such as power supply, collection of rubbish, and transport. When the city floods, these services are badly affected. The first defences built to prevent flooding along the Buriganga were walled **embankments**. These were built in the 1880s. More recently the city has built canals and installed pumps to take water away from the city. However, Dhaka has been struck by several bad floods that have crippled the city. The bad floods in 1998 and 2004 happened when heavy monsoon rains coincided with high tides that forced seawater onto the land. Flood defences failed as water broke through embankments and electrical pumps failed.

# Living in Dhaka

Dhaka is a **megacity** because more than 10 million people live there. In 2000, it had the 11th biggest city population in the world. In 2025 it is likely to be the largest of all. What is remarkable about this city is its speed of growth. Since Partition, Dhaka has grown 30 times bigger. This has been achieved by draining and filling in swamp land and river channels on the edges of the city. Much expansion has been poorly planned. For example, only a third of the city has any sewage facilities and many **lagoons** used to raise fish for food are polluted with industrial waste.

Bangladeshi families have an average of four children. A Bangladeshi adult earns around £300 ($500) a year, or about 70 times less than the average British adult. However, many earn far less. Five million people in Dhaka do not have enough to eat. Poor people moving into the city from the countryside often settle in the least desirable places. **Slum** housing, made up of cardboard and rusty metal sheets, has developed on the edge of the Buriganga and other rivers with no embankments. They are some of the places in Dhaka most vulnerable to flooding.

Dhaka's population is growing by over 1 million people each year.

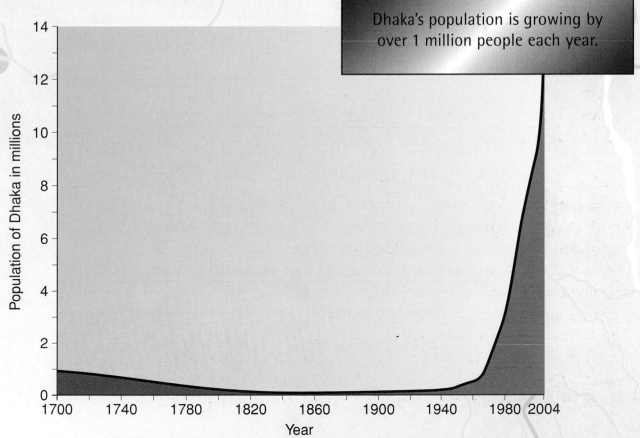

## Changing the balance

The extent and frequency of the natural flooding of the Ganges is being made much worse by human activity in the delta. A natural balance between land and water has developed over thousands of years. When people drain land for building, or create protective walls along water channels, the water simply flows somewhere else. This increases flooding in different areas. In the 1960s, the Bangladeshi government built high coastal embankments to protect homes and fields from flooding with seawater. Then farmers could grow more rice on their land. But tides left tonnes of sediment on river beds and blocked drainage around the rice fields. This trapped floodwater has created hundreds of miles of permanently **waterlogged** land.

Embankments, built to protect fields from flooding, only caused flooding to be worse in other areas.

### Forest buffer zone

*The Sunderbans, where the Ganges and other rivers of the delta meet the sea, are the largest coastal forest on the planet. They help stop seawater surging onto the land during high tides and tropical storms in the Bay of Bengal. The Sunderbans are also home to a unique **ecosystem** of mangrove trees, fish, birds, crocodiles, and tigers. Sadly, the Sunderbans are under threat as people fish for rare species and cut down trees for sale as timber.*

**1608**

City established by Mughal emperor.

**1765**

British East India Company takes over Dhaka.

# Water problems

The delta is also being seriously affected by human activity on the Ganges further upstream. In the Himalayas there is major **deforestation** of the mountain slopes as people cut trees for timber or to clear land for farming and building. When slopes are bare, the surface soil is more easily washed into the river by rainwater. The Ganges, and its mountain tributaries, carry more and more of this sediment each year. Dams and canals built for **irrigating** the upper and middle reaches have greatly reduced the amount of Ganges riverwater entering the delta. The Ganges moves more slowly and is less able to wash sediment through the delta out to sea. Instead the sediment collects and obstructs the flow of water through the delta.

As there is less water coming down the rivers, seawater from the Bay of Bengal is pushing further inland up rivers. So, salt water spoils drinking water supplies and floods fields, ruining crops that cannot grow in salty soil. As a result more farmers leave the countryside to go to the big cities, such as Dhaka, to look for work.

Sediment washed down the Ganges into the Bhadra river, south of Dhaka, has blocked it up so much it cannot provide enough water to irrigate rice fields along its banks, or allow navigation along its course.

| 1905 | 1971 | 2004 |
| --- | --- | --- |
| Dhaka made capital of East Bengal. | Dhaka becomes capital of Bangladesh. | Major flood in Dhaka. |

# The Ganges of tomorrow

The Ganges, its tributaries and the settlements along its length have a long and fascinating history. However, the river and the people whose lives are closely linked to it face a difficult and uncertain future.

Many scientists and politicians predict that there will be increasing conflict over Ganges water in the Indian **subcontinent**. At the moment there is an agreement over how much water India and Bangladesh take from the Ganges at the Farakka **barrage**, above Kolkata. However, there are ambitious projects planned to divert more Ganges water into India. A scheme in Uttar Pradesh state plans to connect the Ganges and Brahmaputra above Bangladesh in order to divert water through 1000 kilometres (600 miles) of canals and to **irrigate** drier regions of India. Many people fear such projects will cause disputes between India and Bangladesh.

The unfinished Tehri dam in the Himalayas above Haridwar is one possible threat to water flow in the Ganges. The dam will provide hydroelectric power for millions, but will also displace thousands of villages.

In the future, river-borne disease and pollution from sewage may change the ways Hindus can safely use Ganges water in their religious ceremonies.

## Pollution time-bomb

The ability of the Ganges to break down pollution is already being exceeded by the amount being dumped in it. For example, large amounts of the chemical chromium are washed into the river from leather **tanning** industries around Kanpur. This can cause cancer in the people and livestock that drink river water.

### GAP

*The Ganga Action Plan was an ambitious scheme started in 1985 to clear up sewage pollution in the Ganges. Although it successfully brought together many local communities, it is failing. One reason for this failure is that many new water-treatment machines cannot work because of a shortage of electricity.*

## Natural threats

The climate on Earth is gradually getting hotter. This climate change will affect the Ganges in two major ways. First, the Gangotri **glacier** is shrinking by 30 metres (98 feet) a year. In the short term this will increase the flow into the Ganges but within a few thousand years it may start to dry up. Second, as the polar ice caps shrink, their **meltwater** is raising sea levels around the world. This threatens to plunge land and settlements in the low-lying Ganges delta under water.

The settlements of the Ganges will be profoundly affected as the river changes in future. Nevertheless 'Ganga Maiya' will continue to dominate the lives of the many people who live along its length.

# Timeline

| | |
|---|---|
| c1500 BC | Aryans arrive in Prayaga (Allahabad). |
| c1400 | First city on the site of Delhi, Indruprastha. |
| c600 | Varanasi is established as a religious centre. |
| c563 | Gotama (Buddha) born. |
| 326 | Chandragupta becomes ruler of Mauryan Empire. |
| 269–232 | Reign of Asoka over Mauryan Empire. |
| AD319–500 | Gupta empire. |
| c350 | Prayaga is a major settlement ruled by Gupta emperors. |
| 1194 | Muhammed of Ghori sacks Varanasi. |
| 1206 | Delhi sultanate established. |
| 1540–5 | Azimabad (later Patna) built on site of Pataliputra. |
| 1575 | Akbar renames Prayaga Illahabas (Allahabad). |
| 1608 | Earliest Dhaka established by Mughal emperor. |
| 1648 | Shahjahanabad (Old Delhi) completed. |
| 1690 | Factory at Sutanuti built, the beginnings of Kolkata. |
| c1750 | Varanasi becomes an independent state within India. |
| 1756 | Black Hole of Calcutta incident. |
| 1765 | British East India Company takes over Dhaka. |
| 1801–3 | British East India Company takes over Allahabad and Delhi. |
| 1855 | First jute mill built in Kolkata. |
| 1857 | Great Rebellion erupts in Kolkata. |
| 1873 | The British East India Company ends. |
| 1877 | Kolkata is made capital of India. |
| 1885 | Indian National Congress is founded in Kolkata. |
| 1905 | Dhaka made capital of East Bengal. |
| 1911 | British decide to move capital from Kolkata to Delhi. |
| 1931 | New Delhi completed as official capital of British India. |
| 1947 | Partition of British India into India and Pakistan. |
| 1950 | Delhi is made the official capital of independent India. |
| 1971 | War of liberation in East Pakistan between Indian and Pakistan, Dhaka becomes capital of Bangladesh. |
| 1975 | Farakka barrage in operation on the Ganges. |
| 1982 | Mahatma Gandhi Setu Bridge built at Patna. |
| 1998 | Major flood in Dhaka. |
| 2004 | Major flood in Dhaka. |

# Further resources

## Books to read

*A River Journey: The Ganges*,
Rob Bowden, Hodder Wayland, 2003

*World Tour: India*,
Reshma Sapre, Raintree, 2003

*Nations of the World: India*,
Anita Dalal, Raintree, 2003

## Websites

Indian culture
**www.ancientindia.co.uk**
A series of pages hosted by the British Museum in London
covering early Hinduism, Buddhism and other topics about
Indian culture in the past.

Mystic Ganga
**http://library.thinkquest.org/22659/**
The 'Mystic Ganga' pages written by Indian schoolchildren
are all about the great Indian River, from myths to facts about
the settlements on the Ganges.

Threats to the Ganges
**www.thewaterpage.com/ganges.htm**
**http://web.bryant.edu/~langlois/ecology/gangeshome.htm**
These sites concentrate on threats to the Ganges River, such as
pollution and removal of river water for irrigation and the
plight of the endangered Ganges river dolphin.

Empires of the Ganges
**www.allempires.com/empires**
A site that covers some of the empires that have dominated
parts of the River Ganges over the last 3000 years.

# Glossary

**agriculture** practice of growing crops or raising animals for food or to sell

**barrage** artifical barrier built across a river to protect against floods or produce hydro-electricity

**basin** total area of land from which water drains into a river

**bazaar** market, usually in an Asian or north African country

**Brahman** creator of life in the Hindu religion

**British Empire** period in which Britain had political and military control over large parts of the world. At its greatest between the early 17th and late 19th centuries.

**Buddhism** form of religion, particularly common in eastern Asia (e.g. Tibet, Nepal, Sri Lanka)

**civilization** society with shared systems, customs and governing powers

**confluence** point where two or more river channels meet

**delta** area at the mouth of a river formed by sediment being deposited in a triangular shape

**edict** official command

**embankment** walls of soil or stone to hold back water

**erode** the wearing away of rock and soil by wind, water, ice or acid

**estuary** the lower course of a river where saltwater flows in to mix with freshwater

**export** transport goods out of a country for sale

**germinate** when a seed grows roots and shoots as it develops into a plant

**ghat** stepped, stone edge to a river

**glacier** massive chunk of ice formed from compressed snow that has fallen over many years

**Great Rebellion** major incident in 1857 when Indians protested at the rule of the British Empire

**groundwater** water naturally stored in the ground, in earth or gaps in rock

**Hinduism** religion in which people believe in many gods that represent different aspects of Brahman and reincarnation after death. Common in central and southern India.

**iron ore** type of rock from which iron metal can be extracted

**irrigation** watering crops using specially created systems. Normally used in areas of low rainfall.

**Islam** religion in which people worship Allah, whom they believe to be the one true God

**meander** wind from side to side

**meltwater** water that has melted from glaciers in mountainous areas

**migrant** person who moves to live in another place, for example to find work or to get away from danger

**monsoon** wet season in parts of Asia

**mosque** Muslim place of worship

**mouth** ending point of a river

**Muslim** person who follows the religion of Islam

**navigation** directing a boat along a river or across a lake or sea

**nomads** people who move between different places to graze their livestock

**nutrients** food or ingredients in food that help plants and animals to grow and stay healthy. Soils, for example, contain mineral nutrients that help plants grow.

**Partition** process by which Britain's Indian colony was divided into India and Pakistan at Independence in 1947

**pilgrimage** journey to a place that has special religious significance for the person making it (the pilgrim)

**plain** wide, normally level area of land often found to either side of a river in its middle and lower reaches

**reaches** sections of a river's course

**reincarnation** belief that one's soul is reborn in a new body after death

**ritual** ceremonial or traditional practice. Rituals may be religious or cultural.

**saddhu** Hindu holy man who lives a harsh life to prove his devotion to Hindu beliefs

**sediment** solid particles such as soil or sand that is carried by moving water

**settlement** place where people live permanently

**sewage** human waste material

**slum** dirty, crowded, poor part of a settlement, usually in a large city

**source** starting point of a river

**subcontinent** large land mass, but one that is smaller than a continent

**tannery** place where animal skins are tanned as part of the leather-making process

**trading colony** settlement created to allow trade in goods

**tributary** river or stream that joins another, normally larger river

# Index